Waiting in Joyful Hope

Daily Reflections for
Advent and Christmas 2003–2004
Year C

GW00492615

LITURGICAL PRESS

Collegeville, Minnesota

www.litpress.org

Cover design by Ann Blattner

1	2	3	4	5	6	7	8

ISBN 0-8146-2738-2

Dedicated to my 1956 first-grade teacher,

Sister Laura Magowan, C.C.V.I.,

who for over 50 years

has continued to serve

as a teacher in the Church.

Introduction

The title of this book, *Waiting In Joyful Hope*, comes from the prayer after the Our Father during Mass. After petitioning the Lord to deliver us from evil and to grant us peace, the presider says, "In your mercy keep us free from sin and protect us from all anxiety as we wait in joyful hope for the coming of our Savior, Jesus Christ." The prayer signifies the three aspects of waiting for the Lord to come that Christians embrace during the Advent Season.

Three Aspects of Waiting

First, during Advent we join the people of the past as they waited for Israel's deliverance and redemption.

Second, we wait and name God's presence in our present and attempt to identify how God comes into our lives now. Our struggle to name God's activity in our lives (Emmanuel, meaning "God-with-us") sends us back to the past, especially to the Scriptures, to see how others searched for and found God. Finding God at work in our lives also points us toward the future, which quickly spins into the present.

Third, during Advent we wait for Jesus' future coming in glory at the end of time. This means that we live in the "already but not yet." Jesus has already come once in history. He continues to come every day. Yet, he has not arrived in glory.

Celebrating Christmas

In the Opening Prayer of the Mass at Dawn on Christmas Day we state that "we are filled with the new light" by the birth of Jesus. Then, we ask God to let "the light of faith shine in our words and actions." In other words, we ask God to let the light of Jesus shine through everything we say and do. During the Christmas Season, we focus on Jesus' light shining through us.

The effect of Jesus' new light during the Christmas Season is found in the prefaces which launch the Eucharistic Prayers during Mass. Christmas I preface (P3) declares that Jesus is the revelation of God's love for us: "In him we see our God made visible. . . ."

The topic of the Christmas II preface (P4) is the reconciliation between heaven and earth which was brought about by the Incarnation. Born in time, Christ "has come to lift up all things to himself, to restore unity to creation," and to lead us from exile into God's heavenly reign.

The theme of reconciliation is continued in the Christmas III preface (P5). The focus, however, is on the new relationship that people have with God because of the Incarnation. God has become one with us, and we have "become one again with God."

The manifestation of Christ and the renewal which his revelation brought about is the focus of the Epiphany preface (P6). The words of this prayer echo the Christmas theme of Christ as the light revealed to all people. Through Christ, God "has renewed humanity in his immortal image."

The theme of the manifestation of Christ is continued in the Baptism of the Lord preface (P7) with a reference to the Incarnation and to Jesus' mission as God's servant. The prayer begins with a reference to God's revelation of baptism "by signs and wonders at the Jordan," during which God's "voice was heard from heaven to awaken faith in the presence among us of the Word made man." The Holy Spirit, seen in the form of a dove, anointed Jesus as the Christ and sent him to bring to the poor the Good News of salvation.

Design of This Book

This book is designed to help us wait in joyful hope for the three comings of Jesus and to help us celebrate the new light we experience in our lives throughout the Christmas Season. It may be used by individuals for private reflection and prayer and by homilists for public liturgical preaching and prayer. A six-part exercise is offered for every day of Advent and Christmas.

1. The title for each exercise discloses the primary focus for the day's topic of reflection, meditation, and prayer.

2. All of the Scriptures of the Mass for each day are noted. If you wish to examine the connection between the readings, all you need is a Bible.

3. A few verses of Scripture, taken from the gospel provided in the *Lectionary for Mass* of each day, are provided.

4. A reflection follows the gospel selection. The reflection expands an idea or an image found in the verse from the

gospel. It can be used as the starter for a homily or it can easily be considered as a homilette in itself, especially useful for small congregations.

5. The reflection is followed by a question for personal meditation. Meant to function like a spiritual guide for further development of the idea or image chosen in the reflection, it is designed to lead the reader in making a personal application of the idea or image to his or her life. The reader may choose to use the reflection question as the basis for a journal entry. The question can be used by a homilist as a guide in developing a homily, or it could be posed to a small congregation for its reflection. If it is used in the latter manner, sufficient quiet time for reflection should follow the question.

6. A prayer summarizes the original theme of the gospel, which was touched on in the reading, expanded in the reflection, and which served as a basis for the meditation question. The prayer concludes the daily exercise for the individual.

The devout observance of Advent points us to the Lord's first coming in history, enables us to reflect on his second coming in our lives today, and points us toward his third coming in glory. Throughout Advent we discover that we are always waiting in joyful hope for the coming of the Lord.

Likewise, the devout observance of Christmas fills us with new light. Throughout Christmas we discover that we are always bearers of the new light of Jesus through the words and deeds of our lives.

FIRST WEEK OF ADVENT

Reading the Signs

Mass: Jeremiah 33:14-16; 1 Thessalonians 3:12–4:2;
Luke 21:25-28, 34-36

Scripture:
Jesus said to his disciples:
"There will be signs in the sun, the moon, and the stars,
   and on earth nations will be in dismay,
      perplexed by the roaring of the sea and the waves.
People will die of fright
   in anticipation of what is coming upon the world,
      for the powers of the heavens will be shaken.
And then they will see the Son of Man
   coming in a cloud with power and great glory.
But when these signs begin to happen,
   stand erect and raise your heads
      because your redemption is at hand" (Luke 21:25-28).

Reflection: Always, there are signs that the Lord is coming, but we see the signs so often and interpret them so differently that we miss them. For example, after a week of heavy, overcast skies, the first rays of a new day's sunshine variegate the heavens with pinks, violets, and grays and proclaim that the Lord is near. The sun, earth, and moon align themselves in just the right order to create a seldom-seen full eclipse and announce that the Lord is near.

Go stand outside on a clear, crisp winter's evening and watch the thousands of stars twinkle in the night's darkness and proclaim that redemption is closer than we think. And for a few minutes walk by the sea, listen to its loud roar, and watch its waves paw the shore and realize that the Lord is near.

If we really saw what we see when we look around us and realized to whom all these signs point, we would be tempted to faint from fear. Suddenly, we would realize that the Son of Man comes to us as simply as a cloud is blown by the wind across the vault of the earth. By standing up and raising our heads we can begin to behold the Lord in our midst. He is always coming, and the signs in the sun, the moon, and the stars herald his arrival.

Meditation: What are the signs that herald the coming of the Lord into your life?

Prayer: God of heaven and earth, the sun, the moon, and the stars herald your constant presence with your people and the coming of your Son, our Lord Jesus Christ. Remove my fear and enable me to welcome him with great joy. He lives and reigns with you for ever and ever. Amen.

December 1: Monday of the First Week of Advent

Faith

Mass: Isaiah 2:1-5; Matthew 8:5-11

Scripture:
When Jesus heard [the centurion], he was amazed and said
    to those who followed him,
"Amen, I say to you, in no one in Israel have I found such
    faith" (Matthew 8:10).

Reflection: Why has Jesus not found faith in Israel? After all, he is referring to the land of the Jews, God's chosen and faithful people. But in the this Q story (see Luke 7:1-10), the early Jesus movement is coming to terms with its adolescence, that is, it is breaking away from its Jewish mother and growing up. And, as all adolescents are wont to do, it defines itself by distinguishing itself from its mother.

Israel's legal concept of faith, the keeping of the 613 precepts of the Law, has been replaced with the higher righteousness command of love. The Roman centurion's faith and love compel him to seek healing for his servant from Jesus. In other words, God has already given the gift of faith to the pagan Gentile and he is cooperating with it!

God makes the first move—not us. God offers us God's grace which enables us to respond to God's offer of more grace. That's a difficult concept to keep in mind. Faith, like that of the centurion, is best defined as cooperation with

God. God offers the gift of faith and we cooperate by getting ourselves out of the way so that God can move and direct our lives. If a pagan Roman centurion can do it, then so can we.

Meditation: What role does cooperation with God have in your definition of faith?

Prayer: God of all nations, in your own way you offer your gift of faith to all people. Help me to cooperate with you as I wait in joyful hope for the coming of your Son, Jesus Christ. Amen.

Unity

Mass: Isaiah 11:1-10; Luke 10:21-24

Scripture:
[Jesus said:]
"All things have been handed over to me by my Father.
No one knows who the Son is except the Father,
 and who the Father is except the Son
and anyone to whom the Son wishes to reveal him"
 (Luke 10:22).

Reflection: Luke 10:22 sounds more like the Johannine Jesus than the synoptic Jesus. But this Q saying (see Matthew 11:27), portrays the postresurrected Jesus speaking about possessing all things from God. It represents the Church's reflection on the relationship of unity between God and Jesus before it was defined by the Council of Nicaea in 325 C.E.

The Q reflection tells us that God and Jesus, who know each other, are in relationship with each other. That means, as it does in any human relationship, that they reveal themselves to each other and to whomever each chooses. We do well to keep in mind that Jesus showed us who God is like, since we cannot know who God is! And the God Jesus revealed upset many people, because Jesus' picture of God was not their image of God.

The Lukan Jesus says that God is like one who seeks us when we stray. To demonstrate that metaphor he told the story of the Prodigal Son. God is like one who shows us compassion when we hurt. To enliven that metaphor he narrated the story of the Good Samaritan. And God is like one who loves us when we think that we are unlovable. Jesus demonstrated love by touching lepers and healing the ill. In other words, Jesus reveals that there are no limits to what God is like. And we do well to remember that. Since we cannot know who God is, all we can do is speak about what/who God is like.

Meditation: What do your human relationships reveal about what/who God is like?

Prayer: Eternal God, through Jesus, you have revealed yourself as Father, Son, and Spirit. Draw me deeper into your relationship of love and enable me to do your will until I enter your reign. You are God for ever and ever. Amen.

Compassion

Mass: Isaiah 25:6-10; Matthew 15:29-37

Scripture:
Jesus summoned his disciples and said,
 "My heart is moved with pity for the crowd,
 for they have been with me now for three days
 and have nothing to eat.
I do not want to send them away hungry,
 for fear they may collapse on the way" (Matthew 15:32).

Reflection: When we use the word "compassion," we usu-ally mean sympathy or sorrow for the sufferings or trouble of another accompanied with the urge to help. When the Matthean Jesus says that he has compassion for the crowd, however, he is using a Greek word that carries the connota-tion of "feeling from the gut," or "being moved from within one's bowels." Thus, Jesus' compassion for the hungry crowd emerges from deep within him.

It is the same feeling that washes over us when we see children on the evening news begging for food after a war or a natural disaster. The bony limbs and sagging skin and big eyes move us from deep within ourselves. And if our compassion is genuine, we write a check to the charity that will assist us in feeding such children.

Likewise, compassion can be called forth for homeless street people, the jobless, the uneducated, the depressed. Moved from deep within us, we not only help them realize that God has not abandoned them, but neither have we. Assisting an organization that shelters the homeless and finds work for the jobless, educates the uneducated, and counsels the depressed are means through which we demonstrate compassion.

The crowd that had been with Jesus for three days witnessed a theophany, a manifestation of God through Jesus. God is all over the place in the story of Jesus feeding four thousand, as can be seen by the sacred number of baskets of leftovers—seven. Likewise, God is discovered in our compassionate efforts.

Meditation: For whom have you recently felt compassion? How was God revealed?

Prayer: God of all compassion, from the hidden depths of yourself you shared your only Son, Jesus Christ, with the world. May his example enable me to offer compassion to those I meet this day. I make this prayer in his name, for he is Lord for ever and ever. Amen.

December 4: Thursday of the First Week of Advent

Sand

Mass: Isaiah 26:1-6; Matthew 7:21, 24-27

Scripture:
[Jesus said:]
". . . Everyone who listens to these words of mine
　　but does not act on them
　　will be like a fool who built his house on sand.
The rain fell, the floods came,
　　and the winds blew and buffeted the house.
And it collapsed and was completely ruined"
　　(Matthew 7:26-27).

Reflection: Only a fool would build a house on sand. At least that's what Jesus says at the end of the Sermon on the Mount. Not too long ago, we watched TV pictures of fools' oceanfront property pounded by high waves disappear with the outgoing tide. Both the *El Niño* and *La Niña* phenomena left sandy cliffs crumbling as water washed away foundations and houses tumbled into the ocean. What took years to build was gone as fast as a grain of sand in a tornado.

According to the Matthean Jesus, there is more to following him than just listening to his words. Living, practice, is also required, and that is not built upon sand. The living that Jesus requires in Matthew's Gospel is best characterized as a higher righteousness. Those who follow him are told repeatedly to do the right thing because it is the right thing to do. Law is not the motivator; love is.

And if we are motivated by love, then we don't build on sand, but on rock. The solidity of love enables us to reach outward to the hungry, the thirsty, the stranger, the naked, the sick, and the imprisoned (see Matthew 25:31-46). Any brother or sister who is in need deserves our care because we know it is the right thing to do. As the Matthean Jesus makes clear, ". . . Whatever you did for one of the least brothers [or sisters] of mine, you did for me" (Matthew 25:40).

Meditation: What has been your most recent experience of being foolish, of building on sand?

Prayer: God, my rock, when the floods of life begin to wash the sand from under my feet, help me to realize that you are with me, supporting and strengthening me. Enable me to hear Jesus' word of love and act on it throughout my life. I ask this in his name, for he is Lord for ever and ever. Amen.

December 5: Friday of the First Week of Advent

Spread the News

Mass: Isaiah 29:17-24; Matthew 9:27-31

Scripture:
[The two formerly blind men] . . . went out and spread
  word of [Jesus] through all that land (Matthew 9:31).

Reflection: In the electronic age in which we live, we have
plenty of means to spread the news. Morning news, noon
news, and evening news on the TV, along with the Internet,
radio, and newspaper and magazines enable the spreading
of news. With all the technology at our disposal we can
spread news around the globe in a matter of minutes.

Each of us, in his or her own way, spreads news. If you've
ever won a prize, you know how quickly you had to spread
the news of your winning. If you've come out of surgery
better than before, you told everyone who came to visit you
or called you on the telephone your good news. Even when
you finish a home-improvement project, you tell the news,
like the formerly blind men in Matthew's Gospel whom
Jesus told not to tell what had happened to them.

What we find difficult to contain is the Good News of
what God is doing in our lives. That's what the formerly
blind men experienced. So, despite Jesus' warning, which
Matthew copied from Mark's Gospel (8:26), both blind men
spread the news throughout the area where they live. We

are compelled to tell of the healing, prodding, pulling, tugging that God works within us. Once we become aware of God's work in us, the desire to share our Good News overwhelms us, and we tell all.

Meditation: What recent Good News of God at work in your life did you have to tell? Whom did you tell?

Prayer: God of Good News, through your own words you spread the news of creation and life. In the fullness of time, you delivered more good news in the person of your Son, Jesus Christ. Help me to share the Good News of his coming with all whom I meet. I ask this through Christ the Lord. Amen.

Lost Sheep

Mass: Isaiah 30:19-21, 23-26; Matthew 9:35–10:1, 6-8

Scripture:
Jesus sent out these twelve after instructing them thus,
  "Go to the lost sheep of the house of Israel.
As you go, make this proclamation: 'The Kingdom of
  heaven is at hand'" (Matthew 10:5-7).

Reflection: We are not capable of determining whether the historical Jesus ever told his disciples to take his mission only to the lost sheep of the house of Israel. If he did, that means that he saw his mission as a reform of Judaism. But what the author of Matthew's Gospel—and the others, too—knew was that both Gentiles and Samaritans had accepted Jesus as the Messiah, and that in itself meant that Jesus had to be portrayed as ministering to Gentiles and Samaritans—no matter whether the Jesus of history ever did or didn't.

Gentiles, noncircumcised, non-Jews, are represented in Matthew's Gospel by such people as the Roman centurion, who requests that Jesus heal his servant (Matthew 8:5-14); the Canaanite woman who wants Jesus to heal her daughter (Matthew 15:21-28); and the centurion at the foot of the cross who declares Jesus to be God's Son (Matthew 27:54).

In all three cases, each person is declared to have faith, which motivates him or her to seek or recognize Jesus.

But not even Jewish Matthew can bring himself to give examples of Jesus ministering to Samaritans, those Jews who had intermarried with the Assyrians after they had conquered the northern kingdom in 723 B.C.E. We have to wait for the Lukan Jesus' parable of the Good Samaritan (Luke 10:25-37) and the Samaritan leper healed by Jesus (Luke 17:11-19) and the Johannine narrative about Jesus visiting with a Samaritan woman at a well (John 4:1-42).

While he doesn't do it well, the author of Matthew's Gospel manages to see that Jesus sends his followers to proclaim the Good News of God's reign to all people—no matter what their religious or ethnic designation. At the end of Matthew's Gospel, Jesus tells his disciples, "Go . . . and make disciples of all nations . . ." (Matthew 28:19). That's a difficult lesson—one it seems that we have still to learn.

Meditation: In what ways do you continue Jesus' mission to make disciples of all people?

Prayer: God of all nations and people, your Son entrusted to his followers the Good News of your reign. As one of his disciples, enable me to tell the world about your domain, where you live for ever and ever. Amen.

SECOND WEEK OF ADVENT

December 7: Second Sunday of Advent

The Word of God

Mass: Baruch 5:1-9; Philippians 1:4-6, 8-11; Luke 3:1-6

Scripture:
In the fifteenth year of the reign of Tiberius Caesar,
   when Pontius Pilate was governor of Judea,
   and Herod was tetrarch of Galilee,
   and his brother Philip tetrarch of the region of Ituraea
     and Trachonitis,
   and Lysanias was tetrarch of Abilene,
   during the high priesthood of Annas and Caiaphas,
   the word of God came to John the son of Zechariah in
     the desert (Luke 3:1-2).

Reflection: The author of Luke's Gospel situates the word of God in history when he mentions the rulers of the world at the time that John the Baptist heard God's word. For generations before Jesus was born, God had been speaking his word. Jesus was the incarnate Word of God, the enfleshment of God's speaking. That, however, does not limit God's word.

God continues to speak in our history, our time, today. The Word of God is heard through the voice of a person who calls us to compassion. When we show care and concern for relatives when someone has died, we have heard the Word of God. A fresh idea that seems to come from nowhere can be the voice of God that has been heard. Reading the Bible and listening for a message of application to our lives is another way that God speaks today.

In order to preach the Good News that the kingdom of God is near does not mean that we must have a pulpit in which to stand. No, the best preacher is the one who, like John the Baptist, goes to the wilderness and listens. Only after hearing the word of God does he or she dare to attempt to put into human words what he or she has heard.

Meditation: What word of God have you most recently heard?

Prayer: God of John the Baptist, your prophet listened to your voice and began preparing the way for the coming of your Son, the incarnate Word. Open my ears to hear you as I prepare for the coming of Jesus Christ, who is Lord for ever and ever. Amen.

Holy Spirit

Mass: Genesis 3:9-15, 20; Ephesians 1:3-6, 11-12; Luke 1:26-38

Scripture:
. . . Mary said to the angel,
   "How can this be,
   since I have no relations with a man?"
And the angel said to her in reply,
   "The Holy Spirit will come upon you,
   and the power of the Most High will overshadow you.
Therefore the child to be born
   will be called holy, the Son of God" (Luke 1:34-35).

Reflection: The first evangelist to introduce a theology of the Holy Spirit is Luke. This author understands the Holy Spirit to be a life-giver and one who guides not only the decisions of individual people, but the whole community of believers, the Church.

In Luke's Gospel, barren Elizabeth is given a child—John the Baptist—and she, filled with the Holy Spirit, praises the Virgin Mary, whose womb is overshadowed by the Holy Spirit. Once John is born, his father, Zechariah, filled with the Holy Spirit, praises God's marvelous deeds. Throughout Jesus' ministry, the Spirit leads and guides him to the cross, where his last words return the Spirit to the God who gave it to him in the womb. In the Acts of the Apostles, written by the same author as Luke's Gospel, the Spirit reappears in fire, wind, and tongues on Pentecost, and guides the missionary work of the Church.

The Holy Spirit who prepared Mary to be the Mother of God in her Immaculate Conception overshadows people today and continues to guide the Church. We may not always detect the Spirit's presence, but we can be assured that the Spirit is present when life emerges from death, when hope rises up from despair, and when people gather to praise God and find within the Church the power of the Most High.

Meditation: In what ways has the Holy Spirit enlivened you?

Prayer: Overshadowing God, you guide all that you have created through your Holy Spirit. Send your Spirit into my life and direct my works that they might prepare for the coming in glory of your Son, Jesus Christ, who is Lord for ever and ever. Amen.

Little Ones

Mass: Isaiah 40:1-11; Matthew 18:12-14

Scripture:
Jesus said to his disciples:
". . . It is not the will of your heavenly Father
   that one of these little ones be lost" (Matthew 18:14).

Reflection: Every single person gets too preoccupied, too narrowly focused, on what he or she wants, perceives to be right, understands the intention of the law, etc. instead of what God wills for us. In Matthew's Gospel, Jesus makes clear that God is interested that no little one be lost.

We may desire to equate little one with a child and that is true in Matthew 18:3. But the author expands that understanding to include among the little ones those who are humble, of the earth, anyone in need. This becomes clear in the narrative of the judgment of the nations (Matthew 25:31-46). Those who have taken care of the needy—the hungry, the thirsty, the stranger, the naked, the sick, and the imprisoned—have, without even realizing it, cared for Jesus.

Matthew readjusts our lens so that we get in focus our role as servant to little ones and that we get out of focus our own preoccupations with greatness. Assuming the position of servant enables us to recognize the little ones all around us and serve them in imitation of Jesus, who died doing God's will—that no little one be lost.

Meditation: What little ones have you recognized recently?

Prayer: God of little ones, you desire no one be lost, but that all people be saved. Remove my blindness and expand my vision that I might see all people as your little ones. Then, give me the strength to serve them, for in so doing I serve your Son, Jesus Christ, whose coming in glory I await. He is Lord for ever and ever. Amen.

Gentle, Humble in Heart

Mass: Isaiah 40:25-31; Matthew 11:28-30

Scripture:
Jesus said to the crowds:
"Take my yoke upon you and learn from me,
for I am meek and humble of heart;
and you will find rest for yourselves" (Matthew 11:29).

Reflection: In material borrowed from a source both he and Luke shared (called Q), Matthew records Jesus saying that he is gentle, humble in heart, and that he offers rest. Let's explore each of these.

First, Jesus is gentle. Throughout Matthew's Gospel, people and their needs come first. Following this narrative in Matthew's Gospel, Jesus' disciples pick grain on the Sabbath because they are hungry (12:1-8). Jesus heals a man with a withered hand on the Sabbath (12:9-14), and Jesus cured all who were ill (12:15-16).

Second, when Jesus says that he is humble in heart, he does not mean self-degradation. Humility indicates that he stays in contact with real people, with humus, earth, our status as dust. When we practice Jesus' humility, we know that we are last, like a child, refraining from thinking that something is owed us. All of us are powerless. Acknowledging that enables us to declare that God is all-powerful.

And the All-powerful One reveals God in the deepest recesses of our inner core—the heart.

Third, Jesus offers rest—not sleep or a nap. Jesus offers the freedom to live in God's presence without fear, the freedom to live as God wants us to live by following the principles upon which God's law is based—love.

Meditation: In what ways are you gentle? In what ways are you humble in heart?

Prayer: Gentle God, you have shown your love for all people through the ministry of Jesus, your servant and your Son. Root in my heart a deeper love for you and your people. And at the end of my life give me rest in your domain, where you live and reign for ever and ever. Amen.

Elijah Revisited

Mass: Isaiah 41:13-20; Matthew 11:11-15

Scripture:
Jesus said to the crowds:
. . . If you are willing to accept it,
   [John the Baptist] is Elijah, the one who is to come.
Whoever has ears ought to hear" (Matthew 11:14-15).

Reflection: There is no doubt in Matthew's Gospel that John the Baptist is Elijah revisited. In popular Judaism among some groups (see Malachi 4:5) there was an expectation that Elijah, God's prophet who went to heaven in a fiery chariot and whirlwind (see 2 Kings 2:11), would return to herald the coming of the Messiah. In order to convince his Jewish readers that Jesus was their Messiah, Matthew needed for Elijah to return. So, following the Gospel of Mark's lead in presenting John the Baptist dressed like Elijah (see Matthew 3:4; Mark 1:6; 2 Kings 1:8), Matthew equated John the Baptist with Elijah.

Now the stage was set. Act one presents John the Baptist looking like Elijah. Act two brings Jesus on stage as the Messiah. With the sign of Elijah in place, Jewish readers couldn't help but be convinced that Jesus was their Messiah.

We, too, look for a sign. It may be a person, like a preacher, priest, or minister, who heralds God's presence. It may be an event in our lives that awakens us to the God who is always saving us. During Advent, we raise our awareness of all the times that Elijah returns to herald the presence of the Messiah of his God.

Meditation: Who/What reminds you of God's presence?

Prayer: God of Elijah and John the Baptist, you fill the universe with signs of your presence. Make me aware of those who, like Elijah and John, go before you to herald your domain, where you live for ever and ever. Amen.

Beatitudes

Mass: Zechariah 2:14-17 or Revelation 11:19; 12:1-6, 10; Luke 1:26-38 or Luke 1:39-47

Scripture:
[Elizabeth said to Mary:]
Blessed are you who believed
    that what was spoken to you by the Lord
    would be fulfilled" (Luke 1:45).

Reflection: In Luke's unique story of Mary visiting Elizabeth, the author portrays the mother of John the Baptist speaking three beatitudes, blessings or statements about one's favor with God. The first two occur in Elizabeth's declaration that Mary is blessed among women and that the fruit of her womb, Jesus, is also blessed.

The third beatitude occurs at the end of Elizabeth's speech when she declares Mary blessed for believing that God would fulfill what the Holy One had spoken to her through the angel Gabriel. This last Elizabethan blessing establishes the Virgin as a believer. Indeed, some would say Mary is portrayed as the first Christian believer. The apparent irony—found in all these beatitudes—is that Christ has not yet been born. But Luke, who always seems to be ahead of himself in his narrative, clears this up when he portrays Mary with the apostles after Jesus' ascension in the Acts of the Apostles, Luke's second volume, waiting for the Spirit on Pentecost.

Mary is a woman of faith, of trust, that God fulfills what God promises. That's not only what the Feast of Our Lady of Guadalupe is about, but it is the subject of Advent. We, today's believers, are invited by God to trust God. We are invited to trust that God is who the Holy One has revealed the Mighty One to be—all merciful, all patient, all loving, all forgiving, etc. Just like God fulfills the promises the Great One made to Mary, so God brings to completion those the Holy One makes to us. When our trust is absolute, we are blessed believers.

Meditation: What promises has God made to you and fulfilled? What trust was required of you?

Prayer: God of Mary, you are all merciful, all patient, all loving, and all forgiving. Look upon me, your servant, and strengthen me with a faith like that of the mother of your Son. Bring to completion the work you have begun in me, as I wait for Christ's return in glory. I ask this through Jesus Christ the Lord. Amen.

December 13: Saturday of the Second Week of Advent

Suffering Son of Man

Mass: Sirach 48:1-4, 9-11; Matthew 17:10-13

Scripture:
[Jesus] said . . . "Elijah will indeed come and restore all
   things;
   but I tell you that Elijah has already come,
   and they did not recognize him but did to him whatever
      they pleased.
So also will the Son of Man suffer at their hands"
   (Matthew 17:12).

Reflection: In Matthew's Gospel, as well as in Mark's, John
the Baptist's beheading prefigures Jesus' death on the cross.
What happened to the Baptizer (Mark 6:14-29; Matthew
14:1-12), the herald of the Messiah, will happen to Jesus.

Following Mark's lead, Matthew portrays Jesus as speaking about himself in the third person and referring to himself
as the "Son of Man," an echo of Daniel's vision resembling
one like a Son of Man (see Daniel 7:13). As in Mark, three
times does Jesus predict his death in Matthew (16:21, Mark
8:31; Matthew 17:22-23, Mark 9:30-31; Matthew 20:18-19,
Mark 10:33-34). Using this literary technique, Matthew
keeps the reader interested in the last chapters of his
Gospel—to see if what the hero says comes true.

In the minor prediction of his death in Matthew 17:12, the author has altered his Markan source (9:12). Jesus poses a question to his disciples in Mark, but he makes it a statement of fact in Matthew. Jesus will suffer and be put to death.

For whatever reasons—and each Gospel offers different ones—Jesus was crucified by the Roman occupation government which reserved the right to authorize capital punishment. Thus, part of his prediction was fulfilled. Now, we await his return in glory.

Meditation: When have you recognized that your own predictions have come true?

Prayer: Eternal God, you raised to life the Son of Man, who suffered and died for the sins of the world. Strengthen me in my suffering and give me the patience to wait for him to return at the end of the ages. He is Lord for ever and ever. Amen.

THIRD WEEK OF ADVENT

December 14: Third Sunday of Advent

Water, Spirit, Fire

Mass: Zephaniah 3:14-18; Philippians 4:4-7; Luke 3:10-18

Scripture:
John [the Baptist] answered them all, saying,
 "I am baptizing you with water,
 but one mightier than I is coming.
I am not worthy to loosen the thongs of his sandals.
He will baptize you with the Holy Spirit and fire"
 (Luke 3:16).

Reflection: Of all of the many ways that we use water, one of the most satisfying utilizations of it is for personal washing. We stand under the nozzle of the shower to wash away the past night's sleep. We sit in the tub to soak our aching muscles. On a hot summer's day we jump into a pool to cool down the rays of the sun. Water is our home. After all, once we were conceived, we spent nine months surrounded by it in our mother's womb.

Our personal disposition is often associated with water. After getting out of the shower, we feel like facing a new day. After soaking in a bubble bath, we get out of the tub not only healed of our aches and pains, but renewed in our outlook. The summertime pool can turn our grumpy impatience with the heat to an attitude of cool relaxation. In all cases, the water soothes our spirits and fills us with a renewed appreciation for life.

We might say that the restoration engendered by water rekindles our inner fire for living. We retap the source of life. We drink again from the well of enthusiasm. Our energy level rises. We're ready to set the world on fire.

It is no accident that Luke's John the Baptist connects water, Spirit, and fire. John's baptism was for repentance for the forgiveness of sins. It's focus was one getting people focused on rooting out their selfishness so that they could look more carefully for the coming of the Messiah. However, John knew that simple washing in the Jordan River was not enough. The Messiah would have to baptize people with God's own holiness, the Holy Spirit.

Meditation: Other than in personal washing, where have you found water, Spirit, and fire to be connected in your life?

Prayer: God of water, Spirit, and fire, John the Baptist prepared the way for the coming of your only-begotten Son by preaching a baptism of repentance for the forgiveness of sins. Jesus poured the Holy Spirit on me and sealed me with the consuming fire of your love. Guide my efforts in making known to the world your reign, where Jesus is Lord for ever and ever. Amen.

Washing

Mass: Numbers 24:2-7, 15-17; Matthew 21:23-27

Scripture:
[Jesus said to the chief priests and the elders of the people:]
"Where was John's baptism from?
Was it of heavenly or of human origin?"
They discussed this among themselves and said,
  "If we say 'Of heavenly origin,' he will say to us,
  'Then why did you not believe him?'
But if we say, 'Of human origin,' we fear the crowd,
  for they all regard John as a prophet" (Matthew 21:25-26).

Reflection: The author of Matthew's Gospel borrows material from Mark's Gospel which portrays Jesus engaged in debates with the chief priests and elders of the people in Jerusalem's Temple. One of those debates centers on the origin of John the Baptist's baptism.

Jesus asks the authorities if John's baptism came from God or from John. In other words, did God institute the baptism John preached and conducted in the Jordan River or did John begin it? We need to realize that such ritual washing was a common means of ritual purification in the ancient world. The outside cleansing signified an inner renewal and purity before God. The Essenes, a group of Jews who thought that the Temple's rituals needed reforming, moved to Qumran, where they built monastic-like facilities and practiced daily ritual washings.

The point of Jesus' question to the authorities is that it can't be answered. Whatever God does, other than theophanic revelations, is accomplished through people. Thus, either answer is correct and both answers are wrong. The authorities gradually realize the trap Jesus set for them.

We engage in daily bathing, but we seldom consider it a ritual cleansing. But our daily shower can serve as a reminder not only of our baptism, but also of the renewal taking place in us daily during Advent as we wait for Christ's return in glory at the end of time. Furthermore, every day of our lives, God is working in and through our lives, always "adventing," always coming to us.

Meditation: What types of washing do you do daily? How can each remind you of God's presence and work in and through your life?

Prayer: God of John the Baptist, through his baptizing in the Jordan, you revealed your work in the life of your servant. Wash me of my sins and purify me so that I may be worthy of your call. Make me aware of your presence and work in my life today through water and Spirit. I ask this through Jesus Christ the Lord. Amen.

Stubborn

Mass: Zephaniah 3:1-2, 9-13; Matthew 21:28-32

Scripture:
[Jesus said to the chief priests and the elders of the people:]
when John [the Baptist] came to you in the way of
    righteousness,
  you did not believe him;
  but tax collectors and prostitutes did.
Yet even when you saw that,
  you did not later change your minds and believe him"
    (Matthew 21:32).

Reflection: In Matthew's Gospel, Jesus tells a parable about a man's two sons. After the father asked the first son to work in the vineyard, he said no, but later changed his mind and went. After asking the second son to work in the vineyard, he said yes, but never did any work. Following this unique Matthean parable, Jesus makes an application. The elder son is like tax collectors and prostitutes, who responded to John the Baptist and are responding to Jesus. Because of their conversion, they are entering into God's reign. However, the Jewish chief priests and elders are like the younger son. Not only have they heard John the Baptist and Jesus, but they have witnessed the conversion of some of Israel's most notorious sinners. Still, they do not change their ways.

Into this passage, Matthew introduces his favorite theme of righteousness. Throughout this Gospel, the reader is exhorted to do the right thing because it is the right thing to do. John the Baptist did God's will, but the authorities, those who should, didn't believe him. However, those who shouldn't have responded to him—tax collectors and prostitutes—did! Even when the authorities saw that sign, they didn't change.

While we may not like to think about it, we are just like the authorities—stubborn. We are slow to repent. First, we say we don't need to change. "I'm OK; you're OK," indicates our complacency. Second, we say that others need to repent more than we do, because they are worse than we are. The call to repentance often goes unheeded and we go unchanged.

Meditation: What stubbornness keeps you from repenting and changing?

Prayer: God of righteousness, John the Baptist did your will and called people to repentance. Those who answered his call are a sign to me of my need to repent. Grant me the grace to change and to do your will. I wait for the coming of your Son, Jesus Christ, who is Lord for ever and ever. Amen.

Fourteen

"O" Antiphon:
O Wisdom of our God Most High,
    guiding creation with power and love:
    come to teach us the path of knowledge!

Mass: Genesis 49:2, 8-10; Matthew 1:1-17

Scripture:
. . . The total number of generations
    from Abraham to David
    is fourteen generations;
    from David to the Babylonian exile, fourteen generations;
    from the Babylonian exile to the Christ,
    fourteen generations (Matthew 1:17).

Reflection: If we were reading Matthew's Gospel from a Jewish-Christian perspective, we would be immediately alerted to the author's repetition of fourteen. Presenting three sets of fourteen generations is just too convenient. In fact, the third set contains only thirteen anyway! The division of the Messiah's ancestors into three groups indicates a theophany, a manifestation of God. And when we add the numerical value of the Hebrew consonants in David's name, we get fourteen, not to mention the fact that fourteen is a multiple of seven, another sacred number signifying totality, fullness, completeness.

Using numerology, the unknown author of Matthew's Gospel writes theology. He declares that the Holy One has been in the process of manifesting God's self from Abraham to the Messiah. Indeed, God has been at work in the lives of people of the past even when they weren't aware that the Divine was guiding them. God accomplishes God's will through people over time. Matthew understood this and chose to write about it as three sets of fourteen generations.

The same is true for us today. God works in us even when we are not aware. We may have spoken a kind word to a coworker, let another driver in front of us during rush hour, given a generous donation to a local organization that assists the homeless. At the time, we were just being nice. But with some reflection and hindsight, we may begin to see how God was at work in our lives accomplishing the divine will.

Meditation: What do you think God has recently accomplished in your life to further the divine will?

Prayer: God of all generations, you have never ceased to bring about your will through people. Guide me and bring to fulfillment the good work which you have begun in me. Help me to wait in joyful hope for the coming of the Savior, Jesus Christ, who is Lord for ever and ever. Amen.

Yahweh Saves

"O" Antiphon:
O Leader of the House of Israel,
> giver of the Law to Moses on Sinai:
> come to rescue us with your mighty power!

Mass: Jeremiah 23:5-8; Matthew 1:18-25

Scripture:
[The angel of the Lord said to Joseph,]
"[Mary] will bear a son and you are to name him Jesus
> because he will save his people from their sins"
>> (Matthew 1:21).

Reflection: When the angel of the Lord—a phrase indicating divine revelation—appears to Joseph engaged to Mary, the angel tells him that he is to name the child conceived by the Holy Spirit in Mary's womb Jesus. In Hebrew, Jesus is rendered Joshua and means Yahweh helps or saves.

Joshua was Moses' second in command during the Exodus. After Moses' death on Mount Nebo, Joshua assumed leadership of the people of Israel and led them across the Jordan River and into the Promised Land. Joshua, like Moses before him, is credited with helping the escaped slaves many times.

By the first century C.E. the name Joshua meant Yahweh saves. That's why Mary's child is named Joshua (Jesus) because he represents the culmination of God's history of both helping and saving the chosen people. Indeed, God helped the Hebrews escape Egyptian slavery. God helped the Israelites conquer their enemies and take the Promised Land. Even when they went into Babylonian captivity, God brought the Jews home.

The birth of Jesus represents the enfleshment of God's helping and saving history which continues today through members of Christ's Body. Offering a helping hand to an elderly neighbor, saving a child from hunger, or tutoring the illiterate bestow upon us the name Jesus and represent God's ongoing activity in time.

Meditation: From what has God recently saved you? Who was Jesus for you?

Prayer: Saving God, you never forsake your people. Rescue me from all harm even as you help me to be the hands and feet of your Christ, who has saved me from death through his resurrection. Hear my prayer through Jesus, who is Lord for ever and ever. Amen.

December 19: Friday of the Third Week of Advent

Mute Zechariah

"O" Antiphon:
O Root of Jesse's stem,
  sign of God's love for all his people:
  come to save us without delay!

Mass: Judges 13:2-7, 24-25; Luke 1:5-25

Scripture:
. . . Zechariah said to the angel,
  "How shall I know this?
For I am an old man, and my wife is advanced in years."
And the angel said to him in reply,
  "I am Gabriel, who stand before God.
I was sent to speak to you and to announce to you this
    good news.
But now you will be speechless and unable to talk
  until the day these things take place,
  because you did not believe my words,
  which will be fulfilled at their proper time" (Luke 1:18-20).

Reflection: Zechariah, the father of John the Baptist, knows biology, specifically that an old man and an old woman do not conceive a child. But, as is often the case, Gabriel, whose name means "God's strength," indicates that the God who is always in the process of revealing who the Holy One is to people will continue now through a child who will be born to Zechariah and Elizabeth. The one who serves God, Gabriel, brings this good news, this gospel, to the aged couple.

Gabriel accuses Zechariah of not trusting the angel's words. Who could blame the old man? After all, it's not every day that an old childless couple conceives, especially before the invention of fertility drugs. The angel gives Zechariah a sign, a visible signal, that the good news is authentic: Zechariah will be mute until the child is born.

When we recognize God at work in our lives, aren't we like Zechariah—doubtful, needing a sign, and mute? For example, we experience God through the love of a spouse, a child, or a friend; in the garden; in a sunrise or sunset; in the mountains; on the ocean. We recognize that the person, flower, sun, mountain, or sea is the sign of God-with-us. And we are mute. Try telling someone about your experience of God and you will discover that you are speechless, unable to put into words what you have experienced. However, you know that God is fulfilling in you what God needs from you.

Meditation: What recent sign of God has left you mute?

Prayer: God of Zechariah, you sent your servant the good news of what you were about to do in the world. When he doubted, you gave him a sign that you would fulfill your promise. When I doubt your call, give me a sign of your never-ending presence. Enable me to praise you through Jesus Christ, your Son, whose coming in glory I await. He is Lord for ever and ever. Amen.

Unlimited Possibilities

"O" Antiphon:
O Key of David,
  opening the gates of God's eternal Kingdom:
  come and free the prisoners of darkness!

Mass: Isaiah 7:10-14; Luke 1:26-38

Scripture:
[The angel Gabriel said to Mary:]
". . . Behold, Elizabeth, your relative,
  has also conceived a son in her old age,
    and this is the sixth month for her who was called barren;
  for nothing will be impossible for God" (Luke 1:36-37).

Reflection: Instead of thinking of time as circular—every day repeating twenty-four hours—think of time as linear—infinite. From the linear perspective, the Mighty One is the God of unlimited possibilities which unfold in human time. Of course, this is from a human point of view—the only one we have. From the divine point of view, God is not possibilities but all already exist in the timeless God.

From the linear perspective, the author of Luke's Gospel presents several of God's possibilities. The first involves the old childless couple, Zechariah and Elizabeth. In their golden years, well past child-conceiving and childbearing, what is considered impossible for people is a possibility for God. They give birth to the Messiah's precursor, John the Baptist.

Mary, a virgin, knows that she cannot conceive a child without a man, who, in the ancient world, was thought to carry the child in his seed. The possibility of getting pregnant does not exist for a virgin, but it does for God. The Holy Spirit comes upon her, and the power of God overshadows her, and she conceives and gives birth to Jesus.

As Gabriel tells Mary, "Nothing will be impossible for God." God is unlimited possibilities, as long as we stand in openness to the Divine. When we think of the impossible, we have erected fences: Old women and virgins do not conceive. God, however, has no boundaries. Our impossibilities are God's possibilities.

The last days of Advent offer us the opportunity to examine the fences we erect, that is, our closedness, the circular time we repeat over and over again. Linear time removes walls and sets us on the infinite journey of God's unlimited possibilities.

Meditation: What recently seemed impossible to you and became possible? How was God involved?

Prayer: God of Elizabeth and Mary, all is possible to you and those who place their trust in you. Give me the courage of Elizabeth and the trust of Mary so that I can cooperate with your unlimited possibilities for my life. I await the revelation of your Son, Jesus Christ, who is Lord for ever and ever. Amen.

FOURTH WEEK OF ADVENT

Model of Mary

"O" Antiphon:
O Radiant Dawn,
    splendor of eternal light, sun of justice:
    come and shine on those who dwell in darkness and in
        the shadow of death!

Mass: Micah 5:1-4; Hebrews 10:5-10; Luke 1:39-45

Scripture:
[Elizabeth said to Mary],
"Blessed are you who believed
    that what was spoken to you by the Lord
    would be fulfilled" (Luke 1:45).

Reflection: The author of Luke's Gospel presents Mary as an example of one human being who believed that God would do what the Mighty One said. She trusted God. She stands as a model throughout Luke's Gospel and into his second volume, the Acts of the Apostles, as one who trusts the Merciful One. In fact, Mary is presented as the ideal follower of Christ, a "Christian" prototype.

Mary is a model. She challenges us to wrestle with these questions: "What do we need to do in order to improve our relationship with God? What gets in the way of the growth of our union with God? What virtues can we imitate? What does not need to be changed in our relationship with God?"

Those are questions that we need to ask ourselves regularly. They enable us to clear the way for God to fulfill God's promises in our lives. Just like Mary trusted that the Holy One would bring forth God's Son from her virgin womb, so we believe that the Mighty One can conceive the Holy One's will in our lives.

Meditation: In what ways is Mary a model for you?

Prayer: God of Mary, you called the engaged virgin of Nazareth to conceive your eternal Word, Jesus, for the salvation of the world. She demonstrated the importance of her relationship with you. Help me to imitate her virtue and to grow in my relationship with you through Jesus Christ, who reigns with you for ever and ever. Amen.

Return Home

"O" Antiphon:
O King of all nations and keystone of the Church;
   come and save [us], whom you formed from the dust!

Mass: 1 Samuel 1:24-28; Luke 1:46-56

Scripture:
Mary remained with Elizabeth about three months
   and then returned to her home (Luke 1:56).

Reflection: After visiting relatives and friends, there comes a point when one knows it is time to return home. During the holidays, this is especially true. Our usual routine gets interrupted and we come to the point where we want to go home, sleep in our own bed, use our own bathroom, eat from our own dishes, and relax in our favorite chair. Yes, we return home refreshed, with new ideas, and a different perspective, but we also return to the ordinary in which God is at work.

In Luke's Gospel, the unique narrative of Mary's three-month visitation of Elizabeth is how the author brings together two unexpected pregnancies. While there is no doubt that the Virgin Mary visits the elderly Elizabeth, there is also no doubt that Mary's child-in-the-womb, Jesus, visits Elizabeth's child-in-the-womb, John the Baptist. The kinswomen enable the meeting of the kinsmen.

Thus, the three-month period becomes a theophany—more accurately a Christophany—a manifestation of God's Son to John and to Elizabeth. Once the revelation is complete, Mary returns home to await the next part of the story—the birth of Jesus.

Once we return home, we might reflect on what we both brought to others and received from them during our visit. Don't look just at gifts that may have been exchanged. Look more carefully at how God was shared through conversation, food, and drink. Then, we might also see what the next part of our story is within God's narrative.

Meditation: Whom did you recently visit? What did you share? After returning home, what did you discover about God's will for you?

Prayer: God of Mary, after your daughter carried your Son to Elizabeth and John the Baptist, you brought her home to prepare her to give birth to the Savior of the world. Help me to recognize your presence in all I meet today. When I return home at the end of the day, help me to praise you for all your gifts. Hear my prayer through Jesus Christ, the Lord. Amen.

December 23: Tuesday of the Fourth Week of Advent

Amazed

"O" Antiphon:
O Emmanuel, our King, and Giver of Law:
   come to save us, Lord our God!

Mass: Malachi 3:1-4, 23-24; Luke 1:57-66

Scripture:
[Zechariah] asked for a tablet and wrote,
   "John is his name,"
   and all were amazed (Luke 1:63).

Reflection: A favorite word of the author of Luke's Gospel is amazed. At the end of many of the stories in his Gospel and in the Acts of the Apostles he tells the reader that people were amazed—at what Jesus said or did, at what the apostles said or did. When we are amazed, we are surprised, stunned, awed, caught off guard and are open to God. For those who live on tiptoe—and there aren't too many of them—surprise awaits them around every corner. Amazement is just part of their usual point of view.

Mute Zechariah causes amazement when he writes that he wants his son named John instead of after himself, as his neighbors and relatives want to do. The old man is, of course, following the directive of the angel Gabriel, but he, nevertheless, causes his relatives and neighbors amazement on the day of John's circumcision and naming.

According to Luke, every day holds the potential for amazement. When the divine erupts into our daily lives, we should be amazed. But we get too comfortable in our daily routines and need the surprise of the extraordinary to make us aware of God's presence. So, a friend we haven't seen in years drops by to visit, and we are surprised. We receive a new job offer and find ourselves amazed. The colors of a fall day can catch us off guard. Or the sight of daffodils and tulips during a walk through the yard causes us to pause. In these and many other opportunities, we are amazed. And anytime that we are amazed, we can be sure that God is present.

Meditation: When have you recently been amazed? How was God present to you?

Prayer: God of surprises, you always reveal your presence to your people as they make their pilgrimage through life. Make me aware of you in the surprises of my daily routine. May I never cease to be amazed at all your works as I wait in joyful hope for the coming of my Savior, Jesus Christ, who is Lord for ever and ever. Amen.

Dawn from on High

Mass: 2 Samuel 7:1-5, 8-12, 14, 16; Luke 1:67-79

Scripture:
[Zechariah said:]
"In the tender compassion of our God
    the dawn from on high shall break upon us,
    to shine on those who dwell in darkness and the
       shadow of death,
    and to guide our feet into the way of peace" (Luke 1:78-79).

Reflection: Our God brings order to chaos. The Hebrew Bible's (Old Testament's) book of Genesis narrates how God creates the earth and all that lives on the planet. But the first act of creation is the creation of light and darkness—even before the creation of the sun and moon! Thus, the dawn, the first light of day, is God, of whom the father of John the Baptist, Zechariah, expects a merciful visit.

While Zechariah is anticipating the birth of Jesus, we might apply Zechariah's prophecy to every day. The dawn continues to be a sign of God's presence. Who hasn't been caught up in the splendor of the sunrise over the deep blue ocean? Who hasn't watched the golden light sneak over a mountain top or peek out behind the houses in a neighborhood? Easter sunrise services are held around the world to welcome the Christian sign of Christ's resurrection. Every day the dawn appears and proclaims that God is with us.

Like the sun, God lights our way out of hopelessness, despair, tragedy, etc. God's trustworthiness is like that of the sunrise. We can rest assured that it will take place to guide us to peace, to wholeness, and to holiness in God's presence.

All this is God's work. The Divine shows us mercy, and the Merciful One's kindness enlightens our hearts, just like the sun illuminates the earth.

Meditation: In what ways has God's light shined on you during Advent?

Prayer: God of light, you have shown your kindness and mercy through the birth of your Son, Jesus Christ. As I finish my preparation to celebrate his nativity, make me joyful as I await his return at the end of time. May my celebration of Christmas light give you glory through Jesus Christ and the Holy Spirit. You are one God, for ever and ever. Amen.

CHRISTMAS AND DAYS
WITHIN ITS OCTAVE

Vigil Mass: Emmanuel

Mass: Isaiah 62:1-5; Acts 13:16-17, 22-25; Matthew 1:1-25 or 1:18-25

Scripture:
Behold, the virgin shall conceive and bear a son,
and they shall name him Emmanuel,
which means "God is with us" (Matthew 1:23).

Reflection: The author of Matthew's Gospel is quite famous for his use of Hebrew Bible (Old Testament) quotations or allusions to them. In his unique narrative of Jesus' birth, Matthew quotes Isaiah 7:14, the prophet's assurance to King Ahaz that God would not abandon the people when Jerusalem was under attack by two rival kings. The sign God gave was the promise of Ahaz's son, the future king Hezekiah, who would represent God's presence with the chosen people.

Matthew stretches Isaiah's understanding of Emmanuel by applying it to Jesus of Nazareth. In this author's understanding, Jesus is the sign of God's presence with people. God has not abandoned people, but become one of them.

We may be tempted to leave the concept of Emmanuel there, but there is more. Emmanuel is not a one-time event—either for Isaiah or Matthew. Emmanuel is an ongoing process. We may be more accurate in saying that God

"Emmanuels," God is always in the process of "Emmanueling," of becoming flesh in us and in others. Christmas challenges us to recognize how God has been with us during the past year. Every time we have shared another person's sorrow or pain, every time we have offered a comforting hand, and every time we have reverenced the human dignity of others, God "Emmanueled," the Holy One was present. Each person is a unique manifestation of the divine presence.

Meditation: In what ways have you "Emmanueled," been a sign of God's presence in the past year?

Prayer: God of Emmanuel, you are always faithful to your promise to remain with your people. Make me more aware of your presence in my daily life and enable me to recognize you in every person I meet. Hear my prayer in the name of Jesus Christ, your Son, Emmanuel, for ever and ever. Amen.

Mass at Midnight: Peace

Mass: Isaiah 9:1-6; Titus 2:11-14; Luke 2:1-14

Scripture:
"Glory to God in the highest
   and on earth peace to those on whom his favor rests"
      (Luke 2:14).

Reflection: The word "peace" is illusive and difficult to define. If you were part of the Roman occupation forces in Palestine in the first century C.E., peace would have referred to the "Pax Romana," the long period of no war and stability that existed under the Roman Empire. But if you were a member of the conquered, then peace would mean freedom from your oppressors.

The peace Luke refers to in his unique narrative about angels appearing to shepherds and singing, "Glory to God in the highest and on earth peace to those on whom his favor rests," is one that flows from grace, God's self gift, which makes people whole. It is no Lukan accident that later in his narrative the crowds hail Jesus' entrance into Jerusalem saying, "Blessed is the king who comes in the name of the Lord. Peace in heaven and glory in the highest" (Luke 19:38). Jesus, riding not on a conqueror's horse, but on a donkey's colt, the poor person's work animal, brings God's peace to the inhabitants of the Holy City.

The personal peace that is wholeness results from a balance of the six aspects of being human. First, the mental refers to our minds, our need for intellectual stimulation. Second, the psychological, refers to our self-image. Third, the emotional is concerned with how we feel about ourselves and others. Fourth, the physical refers to the exercise our body needs. Fifth, the sexual aspect is about gender and relating both to the opposite sex and the same sex. Sixth, the spiritual concerns our relationship with God both personally and through others. When these aspects of being human are in harmony, we experience God's peaceful grace of wholeness.

Meditation: When have you most recently experienced God's peaceful grace of wholeness? Examine your experience in light of the six aspects of being human.

Prayer: God of peace, you share your life with your people in order to bring them to wholeness in your presence. Favor me with your grace, and make me whole. Open my lips to sing your praises. May all glory be yours, Father, Son, and Holy Spirit, one God, for ever and ever. Amen.

Mass at Dawn: Pondering

Mass: Isaiah 62:11-12; Titus 3:4-7; Luke 2:15-20

Scripture:
. . . Mary kept all these things,
    reflecting on them in her heart (Luke 2:19).

Reflection: In Luke's Gospel, Mary is portrayed as a pre-Christian believer. She hears God's word and acts on it. Twice Luke tells us that Mary reflected on what she experienced (see 2:19 and 2:51). Reflecting is an aspect of hearing, and praying is an aspect of doing in Lukan theology. Mary, then, is a metaphor for anyone who hears God's word and acts on it.

Christmas day should find us pondering or reflecting on our own experiences of hearing God's word and acting on it. A simple process for reflecting includes four parts—

observing, understanding, testing, deciding. In the observation step, we pay attention to what we have experienced. In the understanding step, we explain to ourselves the meaning of what we have observed. Then, we check out our own accuracy in the testing step by examining our lives to see if we have learned this once before, how our culture influences our understanding, and how our faith affects what we understand our experience to mean. Finally, we decide what our next step will be. While we engage the process mentally, it is very helpful to keep notes for ourselves or to record our ponderings in a journal.

Later today, choose one of your experiences of Christmas from yesterday or today and ponder it. What did you observe about yourself and others? What does your observation mean? Have you experienced this before? What influence does your culture and faith have on the meaning of your experience? Ask another person what he or she thinks about your reflection. Then, decide what action you will now take. And keep in mind that God is at work in every step of the process of pondering.

Meditation: How is God at work in your reflecting right now?

Prayer: God of Mary, the Virgin of Nazareth listened to your word and acted on it. Direct every step of my pondering so that I may recognize your work in my life and praise you through Jesus Christ, your Son, whose birth I celebrate today and whose coming in glory I await. He lives and reigns with you and the Holy Spirit, one God, for ever and ever. Amen.

Mass During the Day: Grace

Mass: Isaiah 52:7-10; Hebrews 1:1-6; John 1:1-18 or 1:1-5, 9-14

Scripture:
From his fullness we have all received,
    grace in place of grace . . . (John 1:16).

Reflection: After Moses led the Hebrews out of Egyptian slavery, God gave the Law to him as a way of life for the Israelites. The Torah—Genesis, Exodus, Leviticus, Numbers, Deuteronomy—is the sacred book of the Jews not only because they believe that it came from God, but because it dictates the way they should live in God's presence.

Christianity, whose mother is Judaism, sees the Torah as a step in the revelation of the lifestyle God requires. Christians do not discount the Law, but they view it from a perspective that declares that God's Word, Jesus Christ, has surpassed it. In other words, Jesus demonstrated a new way of life called grace by the author of John's Gospel. Instead of understanding grace as a noun or thing, think of it as a verb, the process of God sharing the Holy One's essence or being with us.

When we accept the Holy One's offer of grace, we accept the Mighty One and enter into a cooperative way of life with God. Because we cooperate with God's plan, our lifestyle changes. We no longer live legally, but gracefully. And living gracefully implies that we live morally, doing the right thing because it is the right thing to do—no matter what the law says. Christmas celebrates the revelation of God's grace in the person of the incarnate Word, Jesus Christ, who demonstrated how to live cooperatively with God.

Meditation: Does your lifestyle reveal the legal or the graced way of life?

Prayer: Graceful God, you guided your chosen people with the Torah and enabled them to live a holy life in your presence. With the gift of your Holy Spirit enable me to cooperate with your grace and lead a life worthy of a follower of Jesus Christ as I celebrate his birth and wait in joyful hope for his return at the end of time. He is Lord for ever and ever. Amen.

December 26: Feast of St. Stephen, First Martyr

Endurance

Mass: Acts 6:8-10; 7:54-59; Matthew 10:17-22

Scripture:
Jesus said to his disciples:
> "You will be hated by all because of my name,
>   but whoever endures to the end will be saved"
>   (Matthew 10:22).

Reflection: Endurance is the ability to withstand hardship, adversity, or stress and to hold on to our convictions until the end—whatever the end may be. In the context of Matthew's Gospel, endurance implies waiting for Jesus to return at the end of the age and putting up with a lot of persecution while doing so. You see, Matthew's church had a lot to endure.

Internally, what had begun as a reform movement within Judaism—what today we call Christianity—had attracted Gentiles, too. The author of this Gospel was faced with the problem of trying to keep together in one community people from two rival groups. Externally, even while Matthew was attempting to maintain unity, the first Jewish-Christian believers were moving away from their mother, Judaism, and attempting to define themselves separately from Judaism, especially after Jerusalem fell to the Romans in 70 C.E. The Roman occupation forces wanted all these religious groups to get along peacefully—which never happened.

The division taking place around 80 C.E., when Matthew was writing, is all too familiar to us today. Religion still divides people today. Families find themselves fractured when one member marries someone of another religious denomination and converts to his or her religious affiliation. Adult sons and daughters go away to college and come home telling their parents that they no longer believe the way they were raised. Religious leaders foster division by arrogantly preaching that they have access to the true faith and all others are in error.

When faced with such divisiveness, it is easy to forget Matthew's ideal unity of all believers. But even that author knew that it was an ideal. In the Acts of the Apostles we read how Stephen's faith enabled him to endure being stoned to death because he was perceived as being divisive. It's a sobering thought on the day after Christmas—considered by our culture to be one of family unity—to consider what separates us from each other today.

Meditation: What causes division in your relationships? What kind of endurance do you think you need to practice?

Prayer: God of Stephen, you gave your martyr the grace of endurance through his death. Rain that same grace upon me as I deal with all that separates me from my brothers and sisters. Help me to wait in joyful hope for the coming of my Savior, Jesus Christ, who is Lord for ever and ever. Amen.

December 27: Feast of St. John, Apostle and Evangelist

Race

Mass: 1 John 1:1-4; John 20:2-8

Scripture:
[Peter and the other disciple] ran, but the other disciple
    ran faster than Peter
  and arrived at the tomb first . . . (John 20:4).

Reflection: On the Feast of St. John, Apostle and Evangelist, the third day of Christmas, we encounter the unique story of the race between Peter and the other disciple to Jesus' tomb. The early morning run is unique to John's Gospel as is the other disciple, sometimes called the beloved disciple or the one Jesus loved. While Christian tradition has equated that unnamed follower with John, apostle and evangelist, there is no evidence supporting the claim.

The other disciple wins the race, but he stops at the entrance of the tomb and waits for Peter. It is helpful to know that there was a rivalry between Petrine leadership and Johannine leadership in the community for whom this Gospel was written. Thus, by waiting outside the tomb, the other disciple defers to Peter and his leadership role in the nascent Christian community.

During the days before Christmas—and for some people the days after—we race around trying to find what we need. We shop for perfect gifts. The tree needs to be decorated. We roll our cart down the aisles of the grocery store in a mad dash to get every item needed for Christmas dinner. The children's concert requires our attendance. And the dozens of Christmas cards—or thank-you notes—wait for addresses to be written and stamps to be stuck on them. Such racing around can leave us exhausted when we finally get to the beginning of the Christmas Season.

We need to savor the moment instead of racing. That's what the other disciple did while he awaited Peter's arrival. He peered into the empty tomb and believed. On this third day of Christmas if you find yourself still racing, stop and savor the moment. Join the author of John's Gospel and reflect on the fact that Christmas is important because of Easter, because God raised Jesus from the dead. Your faith in the resurrection can help you realize that you don't need a race to experience a new beginning. All you need to do is to savor the moment and look for all the new beginnings around you.

Meditation: What one moment do you savor about this Christmas? How is it a new beginning for you?

Prayer: God of John, you inspired your servant to write about the resurrection of your Son, Jesus Christ. Calm my mind and heart and help me to drink the truth of this new beginning. I have no reason to race to your Son's tomb because he is with me now and for ever. Amen.

Lost

Mass: 1 Samuel 1:20-22, 24-28; 1 John 3:1-2, 21-24; Luke 2:41-52

Scripture:
Each year Jesus' parents went to Jerusalem for the feast of
    Passover,
    and when he was twelve years old,
    they went up according to festival custom.
After they had completed its days, as they were returning,
    the boy Jesus remained behind in Jerusalem,
    but his parents did not know it (Luke 2:41-43).

Reflection: While we usually think of the twelve-year-old Jesus as being lost in Jerusalem's Temple, we can also consider Jesus lost in the human family, especially in terms of experiencing all that is mortal. Mary's child needed food and drink in order to grow from an infant into a twelve-year-old boy. If we would have known the twelve-year-old Jesus, he would have appeared to be just another kid who was a member of the human family.

We can also consider Joseph and Mary lost. The parents made the annual trip to Jerusalem to celebrate the Exodus, the deliverance of their people by God from Egyptian slavery. They are at a loss to understand why Jesus would stay behind in Jerusalem. In their humanity, Jesus is their son who, when found, obediently goes back to Nazareth with them.

We are often lost. Frequently, we think that we have our lives and our world together. We have a good home in which to live. Our income meets our expenses. Our children are doing well in school. Not too many things are broken that cannot be fixed. Life is good! But then, suddenly, we lose a job, or a child is discovered to have a learning disability, or our home is severely damaged. Then, we are lost in the messiness of life.

The Feast of the Holy Family reminds us that even when we feel lost, God is present, finding us. Luke's unique story about Mary and Joseph searching for their lost child in the Temple prepares us for Luke's other unique story about a father searching for his lost son (see Luke 15:11-32). God is interested in finding us no matter where we are lost.

Meditation: In what ways has each member of your family been lost? How was he or she found?

Prayer: God of Joseph, Mary, and Jesus, you have found your lost people through the birth of the Messiah. Turn my experiences of being lost into the occasions of your grace. I ask this through Jesus Christ, who is Lord for ever and ever. Amen.

Light to Gentiles

Mass: 1 John 2:3-11; Luke 2:22-35

Scripture:
[Simeon said:]
". . . My own eyes have seen the salvation
    which you have prepared in the sight of every people,
a light to reveal you to the nations
    and the glory of your people Israel" (Luke 2:30-32).

Reflection: Once he recognizes the anointed of the Lord, Simeon, filled with the Holy Spirit, praises God. What is known as "Simeon's Canticle" is unique to Luke's Gospel and it serves as an outline for the rest of Luke and the Acts of the Apostles, the author's second volume.

First, Simeon declares that his eyes have seen salvation. The child he has recognized as the Lord's anointed is Jesus, whose name means "Yahweh saves." In the person of Jesus, God has kept the promise to save people. Second, Simeon declares that the Christ will be light for the Gentiles. Indeed, this is the concern of the Acts of the Apostles, especially Paul, who not only becomes the Apostle to the Gentiles, but is spoken of in words similar to those of Simeon about Jesus (see Acts 13:47). Third, Simeon declares that Jesus is the glory of Israel, that is, God is with the people the Mighty One chose. The Holy One's face shines upon them.

In Luke's Gospel, Jesus preaches that God's reign is spread upon the earth now. That same message continues through the Acts of the Apostles. From a Jewish point of view, no one would have thought that the message of a Jew from Nazareth would be accepted by Gentiles throughout the world. Simeon reminds us that God saves as God wants and not as we would expect.

Meditation: What unexpected light of salvation have you experienced recently?

Prayer: God of all peoples, you fulfill your promise through the ministry of Jesus, your servant and your Son. Help me to recognize your light and your presence in the world as I wait in joyful hope for the coming of Christ, who is Lord for ever and ever. Amen.

Holy Ground

Mass: 1 John 2:12-17; Luke 2:36-40

Scripture:
[Anna] never left the temple,
   but worshiped night and day with fasting and prayer
      (Luke 2:37).

Reflection: In typical Jewish understanding, God lived in two places—above the dome of the vault of the sky and in the innermost section of the Temple, called the Holy of Holies, in Jerusalem. Because of the Holy One's presence, the earth upon which the Temple was built was considered sacred or holy ground. Anna, the prophetess unique to Luke's Gospel, is portrayed as worshiping through fasting and praying night and day in the sacred space.

Holy ground for us may be our homes, churches, cathedrals, cemeteries, national and/or natural monuments, mountains, Stonehenge, etc. We don't think that God is stationed or bound within such buildings, but that God seemingly is more accessible or available in such sacred places. And when we encounter the Holy One on holy ground, we are changed.

Anna gives us a clue how to enter holy ground. Through fasting and prayer, we empty ourselves so that we can be hungry to be filled with the presence of the divine. That's what Christmas is all about anyway. God emptied the Holy One's self into the person of Jesus, who preached that God was with us at all time and in all places, making every spot on earth holy ground.

Meditation: Where is your favorite holy ground? How do you enter it?

Prayer: God of Anna, your prophetess recognized your presence in the Temple and in the infant Jesus. Grant that I may experience you everywhere on the holy ground of this earth. May your reign come upon my home and family this Christmas Season. Hear my prayer through Jesus Christ, your Son, who is Lord for ever and ever. Amen.

Unseen God

Mass: 1 John 2:18-21; John 1:1-18

Scripture:
No one has ever seen God.
The only-begotten Son, God, who is at the Father's side,
   has revealed him (John 1:18).

Reflection: Throughout the Hebrew Bible (Old Testament), there exists a prohibition that no one can see God and live. In the book of Exodus, Moses gets to see God's back as the Holy One passes by, but no one can see God's face (see Exodus 33:17-23). Likewise, the prophet Isaiah thought that he had unknowingly seen God in the Temple and lamented that he would die until the Holy One purified him (see Isaiah 6:1-8).

In Jesus of Nazareth, however, God took a human face and revealed divinity in a way that people could comprehend. In human flesh, Jesus taught that every human face is a manifestation of God. God's self revelation continues through human flesh—our humanity. The only way to begin to get a glimpse of God is to add up all the human faces that have ever existed and that will ever exist.

It is with that understanding that Jesus' commandment to love self, others, and God makes sense. Through loving self, others, and God, we form a trinity of interconnections, like the Trinity of Father, Son, and Spirit interconnected through love. Human flesh loving reveals divine loving.

Meditation: What human face best discloses God to you?

Prayer: Unseen God, you manifest your love as Father, Son, and Spirit, and you enable your people to experience that love through their love of self, others, and you. Draw me deeper into the circle of your love and help me to recognize you in every person I meet. All glory be yours, eternal Trinity—Father, Son, and Holy Spirit—living for ever and ever. Amen.

JANUARY 1–3

Mothering

Mass: Numbers 6:22-27; Galatians 4:4-7; Luke 2:16-21

Scripture:
. . . Mary kept all these things,
reflecting on them in her heart (Luke 2:19).

Reflection: In celebrating the Solemnity of Mary, Mother of God, we have the opportunity to ponder the gift of Mary's motherhood. She is the mother of one person—Jesus Christ—who is both 100 percent man and 100 percent God. She is the mother of Jesus, born in Bethlehem. She is the mother of the Christ, the anointed of God, the preexistent Word of God. We honor her motherhood because of the Son whom God begot in her womb. In this regard, Mary's motherhood is unique in history.

But from another point of view mothering God is not a one-time event. Think of all the people—male and female—who have mothered you and awakened you to God at work in your life. Of course your parents mothered you. What about your grandparents? Where there any teachers who mothered you by laying foundations for learning and then getting out of the way as you learned to teach yourself? Those who mentor in discipleship by living a reflective life and encouraging us to ponder our own experiences serve as our mothers.

Once we have experienced the mothering that makes us aware of what God is doing in our lives, then we are able to mother others. Some people become parents and mother their children. Others serve as spiritual directors who assist directees in seeing the outline of God's plan in the events of their lives. The way of wisdom is taught by mothers who, having learned from their own experiences, bring us back to important lessons learned from our lives and assist us in practicing what we learned until we get it right.

Meditation: In what ways do you mother others? In what ways do others mother you?

Prayer: God of Mary, you chose the virgin of Nazareth to be the mother of your Son. Help me to learn from her example to awaken others to your presence, even as they awaken me to your love and mercy. Hear my prayer through Jesus Christ, who is Lord for ever and ever. Amen.

Sacred Place

Mass: 1 John 2:22-28; John 1:19-28

Scripture:
This happened in Bethany across the Jordan,
  where John was baptizing (John 1:28).

Reflection: What is it that makes a certain place, a building, or an object sacred? The author of John's Gospel doesn't answer the question, but does mention the sacred town of Bethany, where John the Baptist immersed people in the Jordan River and they experienced something which moved them to change their lives. What makes a place sacred is the experience one has of God there.

Out on Salisbury Plain lies Stonehenge, an ancient circle of stones. If we walk around the stones, we begin to experience the silence and prayer of the place. And being caught up in the circle's magnificence and wonder, we may discover God in that place.

Entering a thirteenth-century cathedral, we know we have entered sacred space. The soaring Gothic arches seem to stretch us from earth to the sky. The light streaming through stained-glass windows makes it seem like we are walking through another world. And the muted sounds of our footsteps on the stone floors make us aware of how sacred the building is. God seems to live there.

The natural beauty of the sea shore, a mountain summit, a dark cave, or an old gnarled tree can bring us into contact with the divine. And we realize that everywhere is sacred space. All can serve as a threshold, a door opening to God, and an experience of transcendence.

Meditation: Where is your sacred place? In what ways do you experience God there?

Prayer: Creator God, from nothing you formed all that exists and left the fingerprints of your presence upon it. Help me to discover you wherever I am and to praise you through Jesus Christ, your Son, who lives and reigns with you and the Holy Spirit, one God, for ever and ever. Amen.

Dove

Mass: 1 John 2:29–3:6; John 1:29-34

Scripture:
John [the Baptist] testified further, saying,
"I saw the Spirit come down like a dove from the sky
and remain upon him" (John 1:32).

Reflection: In all four accounts of Jesus' baptism, the Holy Spirit is portrayed as a dove. In the Synoptic Gospels, the Spirit descends like a dove on him as he emerges from the waters of the Jordan River. In John's Gospel there is no specific mention of Jesus' baptism, but John the Baptist testifies that he saw the Spirit of God come to rest on Jesus. The dove is a metaphor for God's Spirit. It calls to mind the hovering spirit of creation in the Hebrew Bible's (Old Testament's) book of Genesis. Out of chaos the brooding, Spirit-dove hatches order and new life.

But the dove is not the only metaphor used for the Holy Spirit in the Christian Bible (New Testament). In John's Gospel, Jesus speaks to Nicodemus about the Spirit, comparing it to the wind. "The wind blows where it wills," states Jesus. ". . . You can hear the sound it makes, but you do not know where it comes from or where it goes; so it is with everyone of who is born of the Spirit" (John 3:8). After his resurrection, Jesus uses the metaphor of breath for the

Spirit. As God breathed the breath of life into the first human beings, the risen Christ breathes on his disciples with the Holy Spirit (see John 20:22). In his Acts of the Apostles, Luke employs the metaphors of wind, fire, and tongues for the Spirit. Wind recalls creation ordered by the Spirit. Fire recalls God's appearance to Moses in the burning bush. And the ability of people to understand each other reverses the tower of Babel story. God creates order out of human chaos.

During Christmas, we often see the dove of peace on Christmas cards and in newspapers and magazines. During Easter, we focus more on the other metaphors for God's Spirit. No matter what metaphor we use, we are wise to keep in mind that no metaphor adequately captures the reality it attempts to portray. God's Spirit is not a dove, but that does not suppress the unseen, harmonizing activity of God.

Meditation: What is your favorite metaphor for the Holy Spirit? What specific activity of God do you associate with it?

Prayer: Holy Spirit of God, you brood over human chaos bringing order and new life to all creation. Breathe into me the peace of Jesus Christ, your Son, whose coming in glory I await in joyful hope. He is Lord for ever and ever. Amen.

EPIPHANY TO BAPTISM
OF THE LORD

Death Gifts

Mass: Isaiah 60:1-6; Ephesians 3:2-3, 5-6; Matthew 2:1-12

Scripture:
[The Magi] prostrated themselves and did [the child]
    homage.
Then they opened their treasures
    and offered him gifts of gold, frankincense, and myrrh
    (Matthew 2:11).

Reflection: The unique Matthean story of the Magi searching for Jesus by following a star also portrays them as offering three gifts to the child. They find him in a house with his mother—not in a Lukan manger. And from their treasure chests they present gold, frankincense, and myrrh. In popular, cultural presentation, we understand the three gifts to represent the riches reserved for royalty.

However, in the ancient world, these were death gifts, not baby shower gifts. When someone died, gold coins were given to keep the dead's eyes closed. Incense was burned to cover the smell of decaying flesh. And myrrh, a sweet-smelling ointment, was poured over the body to prepare it for burial. Thus, the Magi are wiser than they at first appear, since they are announcing the child's future. In essence, Matthew has presented the passion and death of Jesus in this birth story.

It is only in retrospect that we can begin to understand that some gifts we receive announce our fate. For example, the gift of crayons and a coloring book may herald the making of a future artist. A person who once received a toy calculator may look back to that gift as an announcement concerning a career in banking or bookkeeping. Similarly, one who enjoyed playing with the gift of blocks may conclude that those prefigured a career in architecture. Matthew was able to announce the fate of Jesus through his Magi story because he already knew how the Gospel would end. It's only from the end of our lives that we can invest previous events with meaning.

Meditation: What gifts have you received that announced your future?

Prayer: God of Magi, the gold, frankincense, and myrrh brought to your Son prefigured his suffering and death, but you crowned his life with the gift of resurrection. Grant that my lifestyle may manifest him to all whom I meet until I share the fullness of his epiphany in your reign, where Jesus is Lord for ever and ever. Amen.

Summary

Mass: 1 John 3:22–4:6; Matthew 4:12-17, 23-35

Scripture:
[Jesus'] fame spread to all of Syria,
and they brought to him all who were sick with various
diseases
and racked with pain,
those who were possessed, lunatics, and paralytics,
and he cured them (Matthew 4:24).

Reflection: The author of Matthew's Gospel likes to use summary statements to end various parts of his narrative. They usually precede and/or follow Jesus' five sermons. A summary statement can be compared to chapters in a book or subheads in a magazine article or even icons on a computer screen or mouse buttons on a webpage. They serve to give the reader a sense of having finished one complete explanation before beginning another one.

We may not consider summary statements to be that important until we realize the role they play in our lives. For example, we use summary statements when marking a birthday. They usually begin with a few words like "Ten years ago . . . " or "I remember when . . . ." We use summary statements when graduating from high school or college, reflecting on what we have studied and been trained to do as we launch into the future. And summary statements are made about the dead by the living. Listen to people during a wake or funeral dinner and we hear all kinds of ways that they attempt to summarize the life of the deceased.

Summary statements mark transition periods in our lives. Each serves to close a part, a chapter, a section of living and simultaneously to open the next. They enable us to look back over from where we have come in our lifetime journey and to look forward to where we might be headed.

Meditation: When did you make your last summary statement? What part of your life were you finishing and what was about to begin?

Prayer: God of all life, you give your people the gift of reflection so that they might ponder their relationship with you along their lifetime journey of faith. Make me more aware of your guidance in my life and enable me to cooperate with you as I wait in joyful hope for the coming of Jesus Christ, who lives and reigns with you and the Holy Spirit, one God, for ever and ever. Amen.

Filled

Mass: 1 John 4:7-10; Mark 6:34-44

Scripture:
[The crowd] ate [of the five loaves and two fish] and were
satisfied.
And they picked up twelve wicker baskets full of fragments
and what was left of the fish (Mark 6:42-43).

Reflection: The account of Jesus feeding 5,000 people with
five loaves and two fish is one of two multiplication of food
stories in Mark's Gospel. In the other account, Mark 8:1-10,
Jesus feeds 4,000 people with seven loaves of bread. Of further interest is the fact that each feeding story ends a series
of accounts beginning with a water narrative. Thus, Mark
4:35–6:44 and Mark 6:45–8:10, most likely represent two series of early oral tradition concerning Jesus' deeds.

Both feeding stories note that all who ate were filled. One
of the author's points is that Jesus fills people with food
and word. After teaching his followers about God's reign,
the Markan Jesus demonstrates its presence by filling them
with bread, the element which he uses to signify his body
during his last Passover meal with his disciples. In other
words, Mark wants us to understand that Jesus fills us with
himself through word and food and manifests the presence

of God's rule. The abundance of God's domain is found in the twelve baskets of leftovers.

Most of the time we associate Jesus' feeding stories with Eucharist. We listen to the Word and we eat Jesus' Body under the form of bread and drink his Blood under the form of wine. But the One whose Body and Blood we share also demands that we look at all those others gathered around the table, for we also share of them. When we are filled to overflowing, we have baskets of leftovers of God's rule to share with each other. The care we show for the Body on the altar must also be the reverence we display for the bodies gathered around it. Together with Christ we share the abundance of God's word and work in our lives.

Meditation: What of God's word and work in your life have you shared with others? What have others shared with you? Did you overflow?

Prayer: God of loaves and fishes, you filled your Son's followers with the presence of your reign as he manifested your presence through word and deed. Help me to break bread with others and hasten the coming of your domain, where Jesus is Lord for ever and ever. Amen.

Calm Winds

Mass: 1 John 4:11-18; Mark 6:45-52

Scripture:
[Jesus' disciples] had all seen him [walking toward them
    on the water] and were terrified.
But at once he spoke with them,
  "Take courage, it is I, do not be afraid!"
He got into the boat with them and the wind died down.
They were completely astounded (Mark 6:50-51).

Reflection: Immediately following Mark's first account of
Jesus feeding thousands of people with bread and fish, the
author narrates the story of Jesus walking on water, which
begins the second cycle of unique Markan blocks of material each beginning with a water story and ending with a
feeding story. Motifs typical of the evangelist appear in the
account, such as the disciples' fear of seeing Jesus walk on
water, Jesus' words of calm, the dying down of the wind,
and the amazement of the disciples.

When Jesus comes walking to the disciples on the water,
he manifests God, who not only forms the dry land at the
time of creation, but who in the Psalms is portrayed as
walking on the water. Just as God commands the oceans to
retreat to their basins, so Jesus' words calm both the disciples and the wind. Like God, Jesus has power over the

elements; he can exorcize them, just as he does unclean spirits or demons. Of course, the disciples are amazed by what they witness, but fail to understand that Jesus manifests God's reign.

Wind is a good metaphor for whatever disturbs us. The gale of an unpleasant encounter with a fellow worker may need to be calmed by an apology. Or the wind of a teen seeking his or her independence may need the adult wisdom that balances independence with interdependence. Or the breeze of changes in procedures might need a few words of support from those enacting them. While we always seek calm winds, we can be assured that Jesus brings God's reign into our lives in many other ways. When we recognize the Holy One's presence, our only response is amazement.

Meditation: When have you most recently recognized God's presence through wind? How were you calmed?

Prayer: God of wind, you calm all fears with your presence. When I am disturbed, send your Spirit into my life with the power of a mighty wind. Enable me to live in joyful hope for the coming of Jesus Christ, who lives and reigns with you and the Holy Spirit, one God, for ever and ever. Amen.

Literacy

Mass: 1 John 4:19–5:4; Luke 4:14-22

Scripture:
[Jesus] came to Nazareth, where he had grown up,
    and went according to his custom
    into the synagogue on the sabbath day.
He stood up to read . . . (Luke 4:16).

Reflection: In Luke's Gospel, Jesus' public ministry is launched in his hometown synagogue of Nazareth on the Sabbath. He reads from the scroll of the prophet Isaiah, delivers his first sermon based on what he has just read, and infuriates the townsfolk. Luke greatly elaborates on Mark's account, for that author simply says that Jesus taught in the synagogue in his hometown and the people were offended by him and he by their unbelief (see Mark 6:1-6).

Many biblical scholars think that Jesus was illiterate, if he were a man of his time. Literacy, the ability to read and write, is unique to our time, yet even today many people throughout the world are still unable to recognize characters printed on paper or sign their name on a document. In the first century B.C.E. only a few officials were literate because there were little use in a peasant culture for reading and writing. But writing for upper-class, rich, Gentile, city people, Luke knows that in order for them to accept Jesus, he must be portrayed as literate.

During the days following Epiphany, we continue to reflect on Jesus' manifestation to the Gentiles. From one point of view, this is oxymoronic. Jesus' own people should have believed in him, but, instead, the Gentiles became his faithful followers. For the Jews, Jesus colored outside the lines, associated with the wrong people, and broke too many laws of Torah. Thus, what began was a movement within Judaism quickly grew up and broke away from its mother and spread throughout the Gentile world. The Lukan Jesus' literacy makes him more appealing to Luke's intended audience near the end of the first century.

Meditation: If a new Gospel were being written today, how do you think the author would portray Jesus?

Prayer: God of literacy, your servants, Moses and the prophets, recorded your words and mighty deeds for your chosen people. In the fullness of time, your Word became incarnate and taught with his words and deeds. As I read and ponder this Good News, make me aware of your presence. Hear my prayer in the name of Jesus Christ, who is Lord for ever and ever. Amen.

Divine Physician

Mass: 1 John 5:5-13; Luke 5:12-16

Scripture:
The report about [Jesus] spread all the more,
  and great crowds assembled to listen to him
  and to be cured of their ailments . . . (Luke 5:15).

Reflection: Throughout the Gospels, Jesus is portrayed as a healer, often referred to as the divine physician by early Christians. Luke maintains this tradition by portraying Jesus healing a leper, as well as many other people (see Luke 4:40; 6:18; 7:21). Because there was no modern medicine, doctors, or hospitals, anyone who could heal was sought for help with what we would today label as general aches and pains. There were few real healers, and lifetimes were nowhere near where they are today.

Calling Jesus the divine physician, however, not only refers to his ability to heal physical ailments like leprosy, but his desire to set people free from all that bound them. The Lukan Jesus is on a journey to Jerusalem where he dies, rises, and returns to God. On the way, he heals by forgiving sins, violating Sabbath laws, associating with tax collectors and sinners, raising the dead, and more. In every instance, his healing consists of removing that which suffocates people in their relationship with God. Such healing, of course, causes great troubles for the establishment.

Jesus' type of healing continues today in those men and women who help us see the bigger picture of what it means to be a follower of Jesus. Somewhere in the world, a Baptist minister preaches against Christian arrogance and enables his congregation to see the truth in what others believe. A Buddhist monk solemnly meditates on eternal truth and brings his followers to a deeper respect for all teachers. And countless people, acting on principles, work to heal the world of all types of violence. In every instance, many times without even recognizing it, Jesus' healing continues to spread.

Meditation: In what ways do you continue the healing begun by Jesus, the divine physician?

Prayer: Healing God, when sin had scarred the world, you send your Son, the divine physician, to bring it wholeness. Heal me of every bias, every prejudice, every sin, that I may faithfully follow him whose coming in glory I await, Jesus Christ, who is Lord for ever and ever. Amen.

Bride and Groom

Mass: 1 John 5:14-21; John 3:22-30

Scripture:
[John the Baptist said:]
"The one who has the bride is the bridegroom;
    the best man, who stands and listens for him,
    rejoices greatly at the bridegroom's voice.
So this joy of mine has been made complete" (John 3:29).

Reflection: In order to emphasize that Jesus is greater than John the Baptist, a problem that plagued the early days of Christianity, the author of John's Gospel portrays the Baptizer comparing himself to the groom's best man at a wedding. The best man's role is to wait for the groom and hand over the bride to him, like John the Baptist has waited for Jesus, the groom, and handed over his ministry to him. When the groom arrives, the best man's function is complete.

Using the Hebrew Bible (Old Testament) image of Israel as the bride and God as the groom, John's Gospel employs the same image to speak of the Church as the bride and Jesus as the groom. The Baptist, as best man, steps out of the way as Jesus, the groom, takes possession of the bride whom John has prepared through preaching and baptism. In John's Gospel, this image reaches a crescendo when the groom consummates his love by dying on the cross.

This manifestation of the groom during the days following Epiphany reminds us of the union between Christ and the Church. But it also points toward our role as best man. We bring others as brides to Christ and, like the Baptist, get out of the way. The author of John's Gospel demonstrates how that works through his story about the Samaritan woman at the well (4:1-42). The most unlikely of candidates—a Samaritan and a woman who had been married five times—brings a harvest of people to Jesus. Then, she who had left her water jar at the well moves to the side, like a best man.

Meditation: How do your evangelizing efforts resemble those of John the Baptist?

Prayer: God of John the Baptist, your servant served as best man for your Son, the groom, and handed over to him your people, ready to be joined in love through his blood. Give me the strength to bring others to him whose coming in glory I await, Jesus Christ, who is Lord for ever and ever. Amen.

Anointed Ones

Mass: Isaiah 40:1-5, 9-11; Titus 2:11-14; 3:4-7; Luke 3:15-16, 21-22

Scripture:
After all the people had been baptized
  and Jesus also had been baptized and was praying,
  heaven was opened and the Holy Spirit descended upon him
  in bodily form like a dove.
And a voice came from heaven,
  "You are my beloved Son;
  with you I am well pleased" (Luke 3:21-22).

Reflection: The author of Luke's Gospel portrays Zechariah, Elizabeth, Mary, Simeon, and Anna—who appear at the beginning of his narrative—as filled with the Holy Spirit. Indeed, Mary conceives through the power of the Holy Spirit, who overshadows her. The unique portrayal of everyone being inspired by the Spirit in Luke's Gospel is meant to parallel Pentecost in Luke's second volume—the Acts of the Apostles. There, the Church is launched, like Jesus' mission was launched, by a great outpouring of the Holy Spirit. By the time we get to the account of Jesus' baptism in Luke's Gospel, we are aware of how the Spirit guides all of the characters in God's plan of delivering Good News to people.

A unique characteristic of the Lukan Jesus is the time he sets aside for prayer. Before every major event of his ministry, Jesus is found praying in Luke's Gospel. Before he is baptized, he was praying. Before he chooses his disciples, he prays. Jesus prays before Peter makes his confession. Before the transfiguration, Jesus prays. Even before teaching his disciples how to pray, Jesus prays. Before the account of the Last Supper, on the Mount of Olives, and on the cross, Jesus prays.

The Lukan Jesus is held up to us as a model of who we are called to be as Christians, followers of Christ. We are filled with the Holy Spirit from the day of our baptism. We are initiated into the Church, the Body of Christ, which is animated by God's Spirit. As we experience the Spirit leading and guiding us throughout our lives, we discover that the best way to make our decisions is through prayer. Like Jesus, we pause to pray before the major events of our lives.

Meditation: In what ways do you experience the Holy Spirit leading and guiding you?

Prayer: God of Spirit, through the overshadowing of your Holy Spirit, your only-begotten Son was conceived in the womb of the Virgin Mary and was made man. Because I share in your grace through the outpouring of the Spirit in baptism, make me a faithful follower of Jesus Christ, whose coming I await in joyful hope. He lives and reigns with you for ever and ever. Amen.

CONCLUSION

You have reached the end of another Advent and Christmas Season. You can put this book away, knowing that you're left waiting in joyful hope that Christ will come, like he came in the flesh and as he comes through the various experiences of your life.

Advent is given to us as a yearly four-week period to focus on waiting in joyful hope, but we do it every day. Our daily waiting throughout the rest of this year flows from the waiting we did during Advent and prepares us for the next Advent when we will intensify again our waiting in joyful hope.

St. Paul, maybe better than any other writer, illustrates our lifetime stance of waiting in joyful hope. In his letter to the Romans, Paul writes,

". . . [S]ince we have been justified by faith,
   we have peace with God through our Lord Jesus Christ,
   through whom we have gained access by faith
   to this grace in which we stand,
   and we boast in hope of the glory of God" (5:1-2).

Christmas is given to us as a yearly two- to three-week period to focus on spreading the new light of Jesus through our words and deeds, but we do it every day. Our daily sharing of Jesus' light throughout the rest of this year flows from the sharing we did during Christmas and prepares us for the next Christmas Season when we will focus again on the birth of the new light of Christ.

Again, St. Paul illustrates our need to share the new light. In his second letter to the Corinthians, Paul writes: ". . . [W]e proclaim Jesus Christ as Lord and ourselves as your slaves for Jesus' sake. For it is the God who said, 'Let light shine out of darkness,' who has shone in our hearts to give the light of the knowledge of the glory of God in the face of Jesus Christ" (4:5-6).

As we conclude our intense Advent waiting and opportunity to spread Christmas light, we should find ourselves at peace with God. But we should also be boasting of our hope of one day sharing fully in God's glory. With that faith we continue our waiting in joyful hope, and we continue to share the new light of Christ.